THE ORGANIC VISIBILITY PLAYBOOK

How Women Entrepreneurs Show Up and Shine without Spending a Dime

By

DR. MARCEA BURNETTE WHITAKER, MD

First Edition

Publisher: Boss Life Business Press

Cover Design: Mauhreen Shakuat

Photographer: Emma Burcusel

ISBN: 979-8-9862782-4-7

Disclaimer: This book is for educational and inspirational purposes only. Results may vary and are influenced by many factors including consistency, market, timing, and individual effort.

Dedication

To every woman who ever hid in the shadows—may you find your light, lift your voice, and shine without apology.

Acknowledgments

To the Show Up and Shine community—your courage, stories, and relentless commitment to growth inspired every page. To my family and mentors who reminded me that visibility is not vanity; it's stewardship of the gifts we carry.

About the Author

Dr. Marcea Burnette Whitaker, MD, is a physician, coach, speaker, and champion for women entrepreneurs who are ready to stop shrinking and start shining. She founded the Show Up and Shine community to equip women with confidence, clarity, and free visibility strategies that work in real life and real business. Her mission is simple: help women be seen, known, and paid—without paying for ads.

How to Use This Book

Read Chapters 1–3 to ground your mindset and philosophy.

Use Chapters 4–7 to map your free visibility strategy.

Implement with Chapters 8–10 (action plan, checklists, and tools).

Celebrate the outcomes in Chapter 11 and take next steps in 12– 14.

Keep the appendices bookmarked—your ready-to-use prompts and templates live there.

Tip: You do not need a large audience or a marketing team. You need your voice, a simple plan, and consistent action.

INTRODUCTION

Your Story & the Call to Visibility

I know what it feels like to be qualified and quiet at the same time.

I was the woman with degrees, credentials, a heart for helping—and a habit of hiding. I sat in rooms where I had answers but didn't raise my hand. I watched opportunities pass me because I convinced myself, "Someone else will do it better." I dimmed my voice to avoid judgment and called it humility. It wasn't. It was fear.

What shifted my visibility journey wasn't a marketing course or a stunning website. It was a decision. I realized my silence wasn't protecting me; it was robbing the women I was called to serve. I said yes to a small moment—choosing me. Then one live video. My voice shook; my hands trembled. But one woman messaged me that day: "I needed to hear that." That message changed everything.

Why do so many women remain unseen?

Because we internalize the myths: You need more followers, a bigger budget, a perfect brand, different credentials. We underestimate the strength of our stories and overestimate the importance of paid ads. We're told visibility is expensive. It isn't. It's a discipline.

The vision behind Show Up and Shine is not to turn you into a marketing machine; it's to help you embody your message, activate your voice, and share your value freely and consistently.

This guide will show you how to get seen using only free visibility strategies—strategies that build trust, community, and opportunities without spending a dime.

What this guide will help you achieve:

- Clarity about what you stand for and who you serve.
- Confidence to speak boldly and authentically.
- Consistency to show up without burning out.
- A practical, 30-day action plan and ongoing systems you can sustain.
- More engagement, more collaborations, more authority—and more paid opportunities—without paid ads.

"Visibility is not vanity. It's stewardship."

—Dr. Marcea B. Whitaker

Table of Contents

SECTION 1

THE PHILOSOPHY OF ORGANIC VISIBILITY

CHAPTER 1

What Visibility Really Means

"Visibility is not just being seen. It's being seen for the right thing, by the right people, at the right rhythm."

—Dr. Marcea B. Whitaker

Redefining Visibility

Visibility is more than posting content or chasing algorithms. It is the disciplined practice of showing up where your ideal people already are, with a clear message and a consistent presence, so they can recognize you, rely on you, and ultimately choose you.

In this book, visibility = Confidence + Clarity + Consistency.

- **Confidence:** The courage to be seen in your truth, to speak before you feel "ready," and to stand in your expertise without apologizing.
- **Clarity:** The precision of your message, audience, and promise—so your people immediately understand how you help.
- **Consistency:** The cadence that conditions your audience to trust you'll be there—today, next week, and next month.

"Your voice, shared consistently, will outperform a budget, used sporadically." —Dr. Marcea B. Whitaker

You do not need a big budget to be visible. You need a bold voice, a clear message, and a schedule you can keep.

The Lighthouse Principle

A lighthouse does not chase ships. It shines from a fixed point, steadily and reliably, so ships can find their way. That is your visibility mandate: pick your message, choose your platforms, and show up so consistently that your people orient around your light.

- Show up where your audience already gathers.
- Shine with one clear beam (your message).
- Keep the light steady (your cadence).

When visibility is steady, people move toward you without being pushed.

Voice Over Budget

Your voice is your most powerful asset—more persuasive than any graphic and more memorable than any funnel. It's your lived experience, values, and point of view made useful to others.

Mini case vignette (name changed):

Tasha, a career coach with no ad spend, committed to a weekly "Coffee & Careers" live for 12 weeks. She answered one question, told one story, and gave one next step each time. By week five, she received two podcast invites. By week nine, her DMs included three new client requests—no ads, just her voice showing up faithfully.

A snippet from her first live:

"If you're scared to ask for the raise, start by writing the raise you'd ask for if fear wasn't driving. Read it out loud. Fear shrinks when you hear your own voice."

"Every time you speak, you teach your audience how to trust you."

—Dr. Marcea B. Whitaker

The Three Dimensions of Visibility

- **Internal Visibility (to yourself):** Owning your story and strengths. Without this, you hesitate on camera and water down your message.
- **Relational Visibility (to your audience):** Showing up in ways that build connection—comments, DMs, lives, behind-the-scenes shares.
- **Market Visibility (to your industry):** Being findable by peers, partners, hosts, and organizers through collaborations, guest features, and searchable content.

Healthy visibility strengthens all three. You see you. They see you. The industry sees you.

The Visibility Equation In Practice

Confidence: The Inner Work That Shows

- Micro-bravery: Speak while your knees knock.
- Self-trust routines: Before you go live, breathe for ten seconds, name your point, state your opening line.
- Courage file: Save screenshots of kind comments and results; review before you create.

"Confidence grows when you keep promises to yourself."

—Dr. Marcea B. Whitaker

Clarity: Message That Lands

Use the One-Liner:

I help [WHO] achieve [RESULT] without [PAIN], using [METHOD].

Choose your 3 Pillars:

Example: Mindset, Method, Momentum.

Every post should sit on one pillar with one actionable point.

Craft a 2-minute Signature Story:

- Struggle: The problem you faced or saw.
- Shift: The moment or insight that changed the path.
- Solution: The method you now use to help others.

Consistency: Rhythm Beats Intensity

- Cadence Finder: Choose 2–3 realistic publishing days/week.
- 15-Minute Rule: Ten minutes to write, five minutes to engage, done.
- Batching: Record three short videos in one session. Schedule them.

Consistency turns you from "someone I saw" into "someone I follow," then "someone I hire."

Minimum Viable Visibility (MVV)

When you feel overwhelmed, MVV keeps you moving:

- 3 posts/week: one how-to, one story, one invitation.
- 10 minutes/day engagement: comment thoughtfully on five posts from your ideal audience or partners.
- 1 live/week: share one tip, one story, one next step. That's it. Simple works because you'll actually do it.

Metrics That Matter

Track signals that indicate trust, not just noise:

- Saves: Your content is valuable enough to revisit.
- Replies/DMs: You're creating conversation, not just broadcast.
- Invitations: Guesting, collaborations, or requests to speak.
- Conversions: Email signups, discovery calls, purchases.

Keep a weekly dashboard:

- What post got the most saves?
- What message sparked the most replies?
- What question kept showing up?

"Measure what you want more of – trust, conversation, invitations."

—Dr. Marcea B. Whitaker

Myths That Keep You Quiet

"I need better gear."

Start with your phone, natural light, and clear audio.

Excellence > expensive.

"It's too saturated."

Saturated markets always have room for specificity. Speak to a slice, not a stadium.

"I'll wait until I'm ready."

Readiness is built, not found. Practice in public makes you ready. "I have nothing new to say."

Your story + your method + your voice = new. No one else has your combination.

Reframe each myth into a move:

- From "I need gear" to "I'll record with what I have—today."
- From "It's saturated" to "I'll specialize and show up weekly."
- From "I'll wait" to "I'll practice out loud."
- From "Nothing new" to "I'll say it my way."

The Ethics of Visibility

Visibility is stewardship, not performance. Serve first.

- Truth-telling: Share wins and lessons—no exaggeration.
- Consent: Ask permission before sharing client details; anonymize when needed.
- Boundaries: Your story is yours; share what's processed, not what's still a wound.
- Representation: Your presence opens doors for others. Be intentional.

> *"Integrity is the brightest filter you can use."*
>
> —Dr. Marcea B. Whitaker

Micro Case Studies

Early-Stage Example:

Naya, a virtual assistant, posted three weekly "before/after" workflow tips for 8 weeks and engaged for 10 minutes daily. She booked two retainer clients from DMs alone. Her secret: simple, specific, steady.

Established Pivot Example:

Lila, a fitness coach, shifted from weight loss talk to strength and longevity for 40+ women. She renamed her weekly live to "Strong at 40+," told one client story per week, and pitched three podcasts with that angle. Two accepted. Her calendar filled with aligned clients.

Scripts and Starters

Opening a Live:

"If we haven't met, I'm [Name]. I help [WHO] get [RESULT] without [PAIN]. Today, in 10 minutes, I'll show you how to [specific outcome]."

Story Post Frame:

"Three years ago, I [struggle]. Then I realized [shift]. Here's the step I took that changed everything: [solution]. If you're here too, try this: [micro action]."

Invitation Close:

"If this resonates, comment 'ready' and I'll send you a simple checklist to get started."

Collaboration Ask:

"Your audience cares about [topic]. I can teach [result] in 15 minutes with three steps. Want to co-host a short session?"

A Simple Weekly Plan

- Monday: How-to post (pillar 1) + 10 minutes of engagement.

- Wednesday: Story post (pillar 2) + reply to all comments/DMs.
- Friday: 12-minute live (pillar 3) + repurpose the live into a short.
- Ongoing: Save questions you receive; each becomes next week's content.

Repeat this for four weeks. Review metrics and refine.

"Strategy wins the month. Consistency wins the year."

—Dr. Marcea B. Whitaker

Try This: 10-Minute Confidence Primer

1. Stand or sit tall; breathe in for 4, out for 6 (three rounds).
2. Say your One-Liner out loud, twice.
3. Smile at the lens like you're greeting a friend.
4. Press record. Speak one tip. End with one invitation.
5. Post before you edit yourself into silence.

Reflection Questions

1. How do I define visibility right now—and how will I refine that definition to serve my goals?
2. Which "C" do I need most this month: Confidence, Clarity, or Consistency? Why?
3. What is my One-Liner (I help [WHO] achieve [RESULT] without [PAIN], using [METHOD])?
4. Which three content pillars best organize my message?
5. What part of my signature story (struggle, shift, solution) will I share this week?

6. What is my realistic publishing cadence for the next 30 days?
7. What is my Minimum Viable Visibility plan (posts/week, engagement minutes/day, lives/week)?
8. Which metric will I prioritize that reflects trust (saves, replies, invitations, conversions)?
9. What myth about visibility am I ready to retire—and what action will replace it today?
10. Where do I need stronger boundaries or more integrity in how I show up?
11. Who can I collaborate with in the next two weeks for co-visibility?
12. What small visibility promise can I make—and keep—every day this week?
13. Which audience question am I seeing repeatedly, and how will I answer it publicly?
14. What will I stop doing that dilutes my message or drains my energy?
15. If visibility felt simple and light, what would I do first tomorrow?

"Make one promise to your future self and keep it out loud."

—Dr. Marcea B. Whitaker

CHAPTER 2

Why Women Stay Hidden

"Silence feels safe – until you realize it is costing the very people you're called to help."

—Dr. Marcea B. Whitaker

Naming the Real Reasons

- **Fear of judgment:** You've seen criticism online and decided it's safer to stay small.
- **"I don't know what to say":** Blank pages and blinking cursors freeze you.
- **Feeling unqualified:** Degrees and experience still don't silence the "Who am I?" doubt.
- **Not understanding the visibility ladder:** You're waiting for a leap instead of taking the next rung.
- **Believing visibility requires money:** You equate reach with ad spend and opt out.

The Psychology Underneath

- **Perfectionism:** "If it isn't perfect, it isn't worth posting."
- **Comparison:** You measure your Day 1 against someone else's Year 5.
- **Over-caring:** You want to serve so well that you hesitate to start.
- **Isolation:** Without co-visibility, momentum fades quickly.

"Perfectionism is procrastination in high heels."

—Dr. Marcea B. Whitaker

Reframes That Unlock Action

- From performance to service: "I'm not performing; I'm helping."
- From proving to practicing: "I practice out loud and get better in public."
- From audience to person: "I'm speaking to one woman who needs this today."
- From fear to stewardship: "My voice is a resource someone is praying for."

The 5×5 Method for "I Don't Know What to Say"

1. List 5 problems your audience faces.
2. List 5 stories from your experience.
3. Combine one problem + one story into a post.
4. Add one tip + one invitation.
5. Repeat weekly.

Example:

Problem—no time for marketing.

Story—your 10-minute daily routine.

Tip—batch 3 reels in 20 minutes.

Invitation—DM "routine" for your checklist.

The Unqualified Myth

You do not have to be the most experienced voice—only a helpful one. Authority is built by showing up with integrity and specificity over time.

Checklist to validate your expertise:

- You've solved the problem for yourself or others.
- You can explain your method step-by-step.
- You're willing to say "I don't know" and go find out.
- You can share receipts (testimonials, case snapshots).

Safety, Boundaries, and Wise Visibility

- Share from scars, not wounds: Process first, post later.
- Use platform tools: Block, mute, and filter comments as needed.
- Create a code of conduct: Your spaces are safe and respectful by design.
- Adopt the "balcony view": Not every comment deserves your front-row energy.

Micro-Bravery Challenges

- Day 1: Comment thoughtfully on three posts.
- Day 2: Share a 2-sentence story with one tip.
- Day 3: Record a 30-second voice note post.
- Day 4: Ask one question in Stories with a poll.
- Day 5: Do a 5-minute live with your opening line only.
- Day 6: DM one potential collaborator.
- Day 7: Reflect—what felt good, what felt forced?

Scripts for Sticky Moments

Handling "Who am I to say this?":

"I am a student and a steward. Today I'm sharing what I know, and I'm open to learning the rest."

Responding to critique:

"Thanks for your perspective. My focus is helping [WHO] achieve [RESULT]. Here's what's worked for them."

Declining misaligned invites:

"Thank you for thinking of me. This isn't aligned right now, but I appreciate the invitation."

Reflection Questions

- Which fear keeps me the quietest—and where did I learn it?
- What evidence do I already have that my voice helps people?
- What would visibility look like if it were a service, not a performance?
- Which 5×5 post can I create today?
- Where do I need stronger boundaries to feel safe showing up?
- What does "good enough to help" look like for me this week?
- Who can I practice visibility with for accountability?
- If I were mentoring a woman like me, what would I tell her to do next?

"Courage is built in tiny reps. Practice out loud."

—Dr. Marcea B. Whitaker

CHAPTER 3

Visibility Is the Engine of Your Business

"People can't buy what they don't know exists."

—Dr. Marcea B. Whitaker

Why Visibility Comes Before Everything Else

Before funnels, before paid ads, before fancy websites—your message must be **proven in the wild**. Organic visibility is your first (and most important) business engine.

Visibility creates:

- **Discovery:** New people finding you organically through posts, comments, groups, tags, or collaborations.
- **Trust:** Showing up consistently builds reliability.
- **Conversion:** When people trust you, they take your next step—joining your list, booking a call, or buying an offer.

The Know–Like–Trust Pathway

Know:

People see you through short-form content, comments, and shares.

Like:

They connect with your story, values, and personality through lives, behind-the-scenes, and vulnerability.

Trust:

They see your results, consistency, testimonials, and expertise.

Map your content to each:

- **Know:** Reels, posts, carousels, helpful comments
- **Like:** Stories, behind the scenes, shared values
- **Trust:** Case studies, live trainings, long-form teaching

From Visibility to Viability

Visibility converts into viability when you have:

- **Offer clarity** (what you're inviting people into)
- **Clear CTAs** everywhere: bio, pinned posts, live endings, stories
- **Low-friction next steps** (free group, checklist, newsletter, webinar)

"Clarity is kind—to you and the people you serve."

Consistency Compounds

Week 1: Awareness

Week 4: Recognition

Week 8: Requests

Week 12: Referrals & repeat invites

Track **leading indicators** (saves, replies, invitations) more than **lagging indicators** (sales).

Micro Case Studies Organic → Opportunity

Deja posted a weekly "Monday Map" for entrepreneurs.

By week six, she was invited to write a guest newsletter article and gained 300 subscribers.

Collaboration Flywheel

Priya co-hosted a 25-minute Thursday live with new partners each month.

Every live brought 20–50 followers and future invitations.

Reflection Questions

- Where in the Know–Like–Trust pathway am I under-publishing?
- What is the clearest next step I want new followers to take?
- Which leading indicators will I track?
- What collaboration can I create this month?

"Visibility precedes viability. Be seen, then be chosen."

—Dr. Marcea B. Whitaker

SECTION 2

THE ORGANIC VISIBILITY LANDSCAPE

CHAPTER 4

The Four Types of Free Visibility

"Your story opens the door; your service keeps you in the room."

—Dr. Marcea B. Whitaker

There are four types of free visibility. You don't need all four at once—but you should master them over time.

1. Voice Visibility (Your Message & Story)

What it is

Teaching, storytelling, sharing insights that demonstrate value.

Tactics

- Signature story posts
- Weekly 5–10 minute audio or live
- "Lessons learned" threads
- Short-form reels summarizing a tip

Do:

- One idea per post
- Speak to one person
- One next step

Don't:

- Stack multiple CTAs
- Ramble
- Over-teach

2. Social Visibility (Platforms, Engagement, Lives)

What it is

Showing up where your ideal clients already scroll.

Tactics

- Weekly 12-minute live
- Commenting on five ideal-client posts/day
- Story polls
- Save-worthy carousels

Sample Week

- Mon: Story-based post
- Wed: Carousel
- Fri: Live
- Daily: 10 minutes engagement

Pro tip: Engage 10 minutes *before* and *after* posting.

3. Media Visibility (Free Media & Borrowed Audiences)

What it includes

- Podcast guest interviews
- Guest blog posts
- Community interviews
- Collaborative livestreams
- Virtual summits

Pitch Checklist

- Timely angle
- Three takeaways
- One sentence credibility

- Clear CTA to book you

4. Community Visibility (Relationships & Partnerships)

What it includes

- Teaching mini-workshops in partner groups
- Co-hosting challenges
- Spotlighting peers
- Participating in industry communities

Principles

- Give first
- Serve specifically
- Follow group culture
- Celebrate collaboration

"Be the person who makes rooms better—then rooms will ask you back."

Putting It Together: A Sample Week

- Monday: Story + value
- Tuesday: Engagement block
- Wednesday: Live
- Thursday: Pitch a podcast
- Friday: Carousel teaching + tag a collaborator

Reflection Questions

- Which visibility type feels most natural to me?
- Which one will I add next?
- What is one recurring series I can own for 12 weeks?
- What is my default CTA for each visibility type?

CHAPTER 5

Where You Are on the Visibility Ladder

"Climb one rung at a time. Speed comes from consistency, not sprinting."

—Dr. Marcea B. Whitaker

There are **five stages** of visibility. Each requires a specific move.

The Visibility Ladder

Hidden: Rarely posting or engaging

Emerging: Posting inconsistently; message forming

Seen: Recognizable; engagement increasing

Known: Regular invites; clear authority

Collaborated-With: Sought-after partner

Self-Assessment Checklist

Circle yes/no:

- I can state my One-Liner clearly.
- I post consistently 3x/week.
- I engage 10–15 minutes/day.
- I pitch 1–2 media opportunities monthly.
- I track my top three metrics weekly.

Results:

0–2 yes → Hidden/Emerging

3–4 yes → Seen/Known

5 yes → Collaborated-With

Moves by Rung

Hidden → Emerging

- Commit to Minimum Viable Visibility (MVV)
- Three posts/week
- One live/week

Emerging → Seen

- Define 3 pillars
- Batch-create weekly
- Create a recurring series

Seen → Known

- Build a one-sheet and signature topic
- Pitch 4–8 shows per month

Known → Collaborated-With

- Host quarterly co-events
- Create a partner playbook
- Build replay + content clips

Partner Playbook Basics

A simple Google Doc:

- Topic
- Date & roles
- Promo assets
- Scripts
- Replay links
- Post-event notes

Reflection Questions

- Which rung am I on today?
- Which rung am I choosing next?
- What weekly behavior supports that shift?
- What recurring series can I own?
- Which three collaborators should I approach?

CHAPTER 6

What Blocks Free Visibility

"Blockers are signals, not stop signs."

—Dr. Marcea B. Whitaker

There are 5 major blockers to free visibility.

1. **Inconsistency**

Cause: Over-ambitious schedules; no system

Fix: Sustainable cadence + templates + batching

2. **Unclear Message**

Cause: Trying to help everyone

Fix: One-Liner + three pillars

3. **Low Confidence**

Cause: Fear of judgment

Fix: Micro-bravery + courage file + practice reps

4. **Isolation**

Cause: Building alone

Fix: Community, accountability, co-visibility

5. **Lack of Plan**

Cause: Winging it

Fix: 30-day action plan + weekly review

Stop/Start/Continue

Stop: Posting only when inspired

Start: Scheduling content blocks

Continue: Tracking saves, replies, invitations

Friction Audit

Time: Shorten formats

Tools: Use free schedulers & templates

Mindset: Replace "perfect" with "posted"

Reflection Questions

- Which blocker shows up most?
- What's the root cause?
- What can I simplify this week?
- What promise will I keep to myself for the next 7 days?

SECTION 3

THE ORGANIC VISIBILITY FORMULA

(THE FRAMEWORK)

CHAPTER 7

The Free Visibility Formula™

"You don't wait for the spotlight – you step into the light you create."

—Dr. Marcea B. Whitaker

This is your signature framework and the foundation of **The Organic Visibility Playbook**.

The **Free Visibility Formula™** is: **ACTIVATE YOUR VOICE**

AMPLIFY YOUR REACH ADVERTISE — FREE ONLY

Step 1: Activate Your Voice

Clarify your message

- One-Liner
- 3 pillars
- 2-minute signature story

Strengthen your presence

Video: eye contact, breathe, land the point

Audio: vary tone, slow down

Text: short paragraphs, bold points

Show up consistently

Choose two platforms you can sustain.

Script:

"Hi, I'm [Name]. I help [WHO] get [RESULT] without [PAIN], using [METHOD]. Today I'll show you one simple step to start."

Step 2: Amplify Your Reach (Free Media)

Everything here is **zero cost**.

Options

- Podcast interviews
- Guest blogs
- YouTube guesting
- Collaborative livestreams
- Summits
- Community interviews

Pitch Template

Subject: Pitch: [Outcome Topic] for Your Audience

Hi [Name],

I serve [WHO] who want [RESULT] without [PAIN]. Your episode/article on [topic] was powerful. I'd love to teach your audience a no-cost framework they can use this week.

Proposed Topic: [Title]

Takeaways:
1.
2.
3.

Warmly,

[Your Name]

Step 3: Advertise (Free Only)

No paid ads. Ever.

Options

- SEO-friendly posts
- Facebook/LinkedIn groups
- High-engagement carousels
- Lives + Stories
- Reels + captions
- Hashtags
- Directory listings
- Tagging partners (with consent)

Mini SEO Checklist

- One keyword per post
- Keyword in first 2 lines
- Clear subheadings
- Save-worthy bullets

Reflection Questions

- Which step (Activate, Amplify, Advertise) needs my focus this month?
- What three podcasts/blogs will I pitch?
- What free "advertising" tactic will I test for 30 days?
- What does success look like for each step?

SECTION 4

THE ORGANIC VISIBILITY BLUEPRINT

CHAPTER 8

30-Day Organic Visibility Action Plan

"Action unlocks answers."

—Dr. Marcea B. Whitaker

This 30-Day Plan is simple, practical, and designed to build **confidence**, **clarity**, and **consistency** all at once.

Each week has a focus:

- **Week 1:** Voice Activation
- **Week 2:** Social Visibility
- **Week 3:** Free Media Outreach
- **Week 4:** Free Advertising Techniques

Do this plan once.

Then repeat it monthly for compounding results.

Week 1: Voice Activation

Day 1: Write your One-Liner.

Day 2: Define your 3 content pillars.

Day 3: Draft your 2-minute signature story.

Day 4: Create your 30-day content calendar (3 posts/week).

Day 5: Record a 60–90 second intro video.

Day 6: Engage for 15 minutes—comment on ideal-client posts.

Day 7: Review what resonated so far.

Week 2: Social Visibility

Day 8: Publish Pillar Post #1.

Day 9: 15 minutes of engagement + Story poll.

Day 10: Go live for 10 minutes (1 tip, 1 story, 1 invitation).

Day 11: Repurpose your live into a reel/short.

Day 12: Publish Pillar Post #2 + carousel.

Day 13: Start 3 new relationships via DMs (value-first).

Day 14: Review metrics: saves, comments, profile visits.

Week 3: Free Media Outreach

Day 15: Build your 10-target Podcast/Partner List.

Day 16: Draft your pitch email (use Appendix B templates).

Day 17: Send 5 pitches.

Day 18: Create or update your one-sheet.

Day 19: Follow up on pitches.

Day 20: Draft a guest post.

Day 21: Submit your guest post.

Week 4: Free Advertising Techniques

Day 22: Research 10 SEO keywords; write one SEO-friendly post.

Day 23: Share a checklist post; invite saves & shares.

Day 24: Teach a 15–20 minute micro-workshop live.

Day 25: Join 2 Facebook/LinkedIn groups; introduce yourself.

Day 26: Record & batch 3 reels/shorts.

Day 27: List yourself in 2 free directories (speaker directories, local business lists, etc.).

Day 28: Invite a partner for a joint live.

Day 29: Metrics review: reach, saves, DMs, conversions.

Day 30: Celebrate wins. Plan your next 30 days.

Reflection Questions

- What was my biggest insight from Week 1?
- Which content format got the most saves or replies?
- Which pitch received the best response—and why?
- What free tactic created the most reach?
- What will I double down on next month?

CHAPTER 9

Your Organic Visibility Checklist

"Checklists build habits. Habits build results."

—Dr. Marcea B. Whitaker

This checklist is your **ongoing cadence**. Keep it printed or saved on your phone.

Daily Checklist

✔ Engage 10–15 minutes (comments + DMs)
✔ Share one mini-value (story, tip, or answer)
✔ Track one trust metric (saves, replies, invitations)

Weekly Checklist

✔ Publish 2–3 posts
✔ Go live or host a Q&A
✔ Pitch 1 media/partner opportunity
✔ Batch 2–3 short videos
✔ Review metrics and refine

Monthly Checklist

✔ Refresh your one-sheet
✔ Audit your bio/CTA
✔ Repurpose top-performing content
✔ Host or co-host one community event
✔ Reassess your visibility ladder stage

Quarterly Checklist

- ✔ Update your signature talk
- ✔ Analyze trends from the past 90 days
- ✔ Retire low-performing formats
- ✔ Revisit SEO keywords and hashtags
- ✔ Plan a collaboration series or mini-summit

Reflection Questions

- Which daily activity moves the needle most for me?
- What can I remove to protect my focus?
- How will I reward myself for consistency this month?

CHAPTER 10

Free Tools & Resources

"Tools remove friction; they don't replace commitment."

—Dr. Marcea B. Whitaker

These free tools keep your visibility simple, scalable, and sustainable.

Design & Content Creation

Canva (Free): Graphics, carousels, covers

Pexels / Unsplash: Free visuals

Google Docs/Slides: Scripts, drafts, outlines

Notion / Trello: Content planning boards

Scheduling & Workflow

Meta Business Suite (Free): Facebook + Instagram scheduling

Buffer (Free tier): Scheduling multiple platforms

Google Calendar: Visibility time blocks

Calendly (Free): Booking links

Video & Audio Tools

CapCut: Quick video editing

iMovie or DaVinci Resolve: Advanced editing

Zoom Basic: Lives, interviews

StreamYard (Free tier): Multicasting

Audacity: Free audio cleanup

Writing & SEO

- **Hemingway App:** Clarity + readability
- **Grammarly (Free):** Grammar + polish
- **Google Trends:** Topic research
- **AnswerThePublic:** Keyword & question insights
- **Ubersuggest (Free tier):** Keyword ideas

Community & Collaboration

- **Slack / Discord:** Host micro-communities
- **Substack / Medium:** Free newsletters + distribution
- **MailerLite / Beehiiv (Free tiers):** Build your list

Pro Tips

- Batch graphics weekly
- Save templates for reels, carousels, and cover slides
- Keep a "Content Bank" in Notion or Trello

Reflection Questions

- Which one tool removes the most friction for me right now?
- What template do I need to create this week that I'll reuse?
- What can I simplify?

SECTION 5

WHAT HAPPENS WHEN YOU SHOW UP

CHAPTER 11

Your Life & Business After Visibility

"Consistency compounds."

—Dr. Marcea B. Whitaker

When you show up consistently, things begin to shift—in your energy, your business, your confidence, and your opportunities.

Here's what changes.

1. Confidence Expands

You begin trusting your voice. You stop overthinking.

You show up faster, smoother, bolder.

2. Engagement Grows

People start replying.

Your DMs increase.

Your content gets saved, not ignored.

3. Collaborations Increase

Hosts reach out to you.

Partners invite you.

Communities ask you to teach.

4. Community Forms Around You

You become a home for the people you're called to serve.

Your platform becomes a **safe space** for transformation.

5. Your Authority Solidifies

Your message becomes recognizable.

Your expertise becomes undeniable.

Your name becomes synonymous with your niche.

6. Opportunities Find You

Speaking invitations.

Podcast features.

Workshops.

Panels.

Clients.

All without ads.

Leading vs. Lagging Indicators

Leading Indicators:

- Saves
- Replies
- Profile visits
- Invitations

Lagging Indicators:

- Email list growth
- Bookings
- Revenue

Focus more on leading indicators—they're the seeds of future success.

Real-Life Visibility Moments

The "silent follower" turns into a client:

"I've been watching you for months. I'm ready."

The "saw you on…" message:

"Your interview was powerful. Can you speak to my group?"

The shared post that brings a referral:

"You were exactly who she needed."

Reflection Questions

- What outcome do I want most in the next 90 days?
- What habit supports that outcome?
- What proof of progress have I overlooked recently?
- How will I celebrate visible and invisible wins?

SECTION 6

NEXT STEPS

CHAPTER 12

Join the Free Community

"Community turns courage into a habit."

—Dr. Marcea B. Whitaker

Welcome to:

Show Up and Shine: The Organic Visibility Playbook Community

A free, supportive sisterhood for visibility-minded women.

www.facebook.com/groups/showupandshineplaybook

This community exists to help women **practice visibility in real time** without fear, pressure, or perfectionism. It is your safe space to test, learn, grow, and shine.

Inside the Community, You'll Find:

- Weekly prompts and writing ideas
- Live micro-trainings and pop-up challenges
- Accountability threads
- Co-working sessions
- Feedback loops and celebrations
- A space to practice going live
- Peer connections and collaboration partners

Community Pledge

We serve first.

We honor boundaries.

We champion each other's wins. We

practice out loud.

We rise together.

Reflection Questions

- How would a supportive community change my consistency?
- What could I contribute to strengthen our sisterhood?
- What do I need to ask for support this week?

CHAPTER 13

Subscribe to the Newsletter

"Preparation meets opportunity in your inbox."

—Dr. Marcea B. Whitaker

Welcome to:

The Visibility Insider

Your weekly roadmap to showing up, getting seen, and shining sustainably—without spending a dime.

www.facebook.com/groups/showupandshineplaybook

You'll Receive:

- A fresh visibility idea you can use the SAME day
- Case studies and real examples
- Scripts, templates, and prompts
- Collaboration opportunities
- Community spotlights
- Mindset + motivation for the week

Sample Issue Structure

1. One actionable visibility insight (under 300 words)
2. One case snapshot
3. One copyable script or template
4. One invitation to practice

Short. Powerful. Doable.

Reflection Questions

- What cadence of learning keeps me growing—weekly or biweekly?
- Which newsletter sections will I actually use?
- How can I apply one idea within 48 hours of reading?

CHAPTER 14

When You're Ready for More

"Grow at the speed of your yes."

—Dr. Marcea B. Whitaker

If you want to go deeper into visibility, business systems, and long-term growth, the next step is:

The Visibility Accelerator™

A transformational experience for women ready to expand beyond organic visibility.

What's Inside (Awareness Only):

- Media mastery (panels, interviews, signature talks)
- Content systems and workflows
- Organic + paid visibility strategy (when aligned)
- Offer positioning and messaging
- Audience growth plans
- CEO-level mindset and structure

This program is not required to succeed.
Your organic visibility will carry you far on its own.
But when you're ready—this is your next evolution.

Reflection Questions

- What signs will tell me I'm ready for advanced strategies?
- Which system needs strengthening before I scale?
- What does sustainable growth look like for me?

APPENDICES

APPENDIX A

100 Content Starters

These prompts are organized by category and designed to fuel your organic content for months.

Authority & Expertise (1–10)

1. A common misconception in my industry is…
2. Three mistakes I made early on—and how I fixed them…
3. A client story: from [problem] to [result]…
4. My 5-minute method for [specific outcome]…
5. If I had to start over today, I would…
6. The framework I use weekly is…
7. How to avoid [common pitfall] in 3 steps…
8. My before/after experience with [process]…
9. Metrics that matter most for [result]…
10. The simplest path to [quick win]…

Mindset & Motivation (11–20)

11. One belief that changed my business…
12. How I handle fear before I go live…
13. What I wish I knew before I started posting…
14. The question I ask when I feel stuck…
15. A "failure" that became a lesson…
16. My visibility non-negotiables…
17. The difference between discomfort and misalignment…
18. How I reset after a tough comment…

19. My 3-minute confidence ritual…
20. The affirmation I use before I post…

Behind the Scenes (21–30)

21. What a content day looks like for me…
22. Tools I use that keep it simple…
23. How I batch-record in under an hour…
24. My checklist before pressing "Post"…
25. My top 3 free communities…
26. A look at my Notion/Trello board…
27. How I repurpose one idea five ways…
28. The story behind my brand name…
29. My weekly review process…
30. A peek into my courage file…

How-To & Tutorials (31–40)

31. How to write a clear, compelling bio…
32. How to craft your signature story…
33. How to pitch your first podcast…
34. How to outline a 10-minute live…
35. How to repurpose content efficiently…
36. How to choose your content pillars…
37. How to set a realistic consistent rhythm…
38. How to use hashtags strategically…
39. How to research your audience through Stories…
40. How to create a save-worthy carousel…

Engagement & Community (41–50)

41. Ask me anything about [topic]…
42. Poll: Which is hardest—confidence, clarity, or consistency…
43. Spotlight a peer and what they taught you…
44. Share your favorite free tool…
45. Ask what topic your audience wants next week…
46. Celebrate a community win…
47. Introduce yourself with a twist…
48. Stitch/duet a helpful tip…
49. Start a 3–5 day mini-challenge…
50. "Reply with 'ready' if you want the checklist…"

Values & Vision (51–60)

51. Why I serve [your audience]…
52. A moment I almost quit—and what kept me going…
53. The impact I want to make in 5 years…
54. What I won't compromise in business…
55. What "shine" means to me…
56. The value that leads my decisions…
57. A change I want to see in my industry…
58. My promise to my community…
59. What success means to me this season…
60. What legacy looks like in my work…

Case Studies & Proof (61–70)

61. Before/after case: [problem] → [result]…

62. A surprising win from a small shift…
63. What didn't work—and why…
64. How we measured ROI without ads…
65. A client win using only free tactics…
66. One testimonial & the story behind it…
67. My most impactful collaboration…
68. A pitch that failed—and the one that worked…
69. The three posts that led to the most DMs…
70. The live that led to [opportunity]…

Quick Wins, Lists & Checklists (71–80)

71. 3 things to do in 10 minutes for visibility…
72. A checklist for your next live…
73. 5 hooks that stop the scroll…
74. 4 CTAs that spark conversation…
75. 6 ways to repurpose today's post…
76. 7 questions for your next poll…
77. 5 reel ideas to try this week…
78. 3 prompts to spark a story…
79. 10 comment starters…
80. 5 ways to end your post clearly…

Collaborations & Media (81–90)

81. My dream collaboration is…
82. Three podcast angles I'm pitching this month…
83. A recent co-hosted live win…
84. What I include in my media one-sheet…

85. Behind the scenes of my media prep…
86. Lessons from my first podcast interview…
87. A panel question I wish I prepared for…
88. How I choose partnership opportunities…
89. How to be a great guest (checklist)…
90. The best "small room" I ever served…

Seasonal & Topical (91–100)

91. What I'm focusing on this quarter…
92. A seasonal tip for [niche]…
93. My take on a trending topic…
94. What I'm reading/watching/learning…
95. A holiday reflection tied to my values…
96. My year-in-review recap…
97. Predictions for next year…
98. What I'm simplifying this season…
99. What I'm releasing—and why…
100. A gratitude post to my community…

APPENDIX B

Pitch Templates

These templates are proven and ready to copy/paste.

Podcast Pitch Email

Subject: Pitch: A 3-Step Organic Visibility Plan for Your Audience

Hi [Host Name],

I serve women entrepreneurs who want to get seen without ads. Your episode on [topic] was powerful, and I'd love to bring your listeners a practical, no-cost framework they can use this week.

Proposed Topic:

The Free Visibility Formula — Activate, Amplify, Advertise (Free Only)

Takeaways:

1. How to craft a 2-minute signature story
2. The 15-minute daily engagement rhythm
3. Zero-budget "advertising" strategies that actually work I've spoken on [relevant platforms].

If this serves your audience, I'd love to schedule a time.

Warmly,

[Your Name]
[Website]
[Scheduling Link]

Follow-Up Pitch

Subject: Quick follow-up on free visibility topic

Hi [Host Name],

Circling back to see if the visibility topic may serve your audience this month. If timing isn't aligned, totally fine—I can reconnect later.

Warmly,

[Your Name]

Guest Blog Pitch

Subject: Guest Post: Organic Visibility Checklist for Your Readers

Hi [Editor],

I enjoyed your recent piece on [topic]. I can contribute a concise, actionable visibility checklist (900–1,200 words) including templates and examples—completely original.

Would this support your readers?

Thanks for considering,

[Your Name]

Collaboration Invite (DM or Email)

Subject: Want to co-host a 20-minute Shine Session?

Hi [Name],

Your audience cares about [topic], and I specialize in organic visibility.

Would you be open to a co-hosted 20-minute session where we each teach one practical tip + 10 minutes Q&A?

Low-lift, high-value.

Thoughts?

Warmly,

[Your Name]

One-Sheet Outline (for your media kit)

- Name + headshot
- 2–3 sentence media bio
- Topics + takeaways
- Previous features or audience testimonials
- Social links
- Scheduling link

APPENDIX C

Journaling Prompts for Courage & Clarity

Use these whenever your confidence or clarity dips.

1. What part of my story is someone waiting to hear today?
2. If I trusted my voice fully, how would I show up this week?
3. What am I afraid they'll say—and what is more true than that fear?
4. Where did I keep a promise to myself last week?
5. What would "simple and consistent" look like?
6. Which collaboration would stretch me (in a good way)?
7. What does "shine without a dime" look like for me this month?
8. What boundaries create safety for my visibility?
9. What question do people ask me the most?
10. Where am I overcomplicating what could be simple?
11. What's my best 10-minute routine?
12. Which metric means trust to me—and why?
13. What courageous ask can I make this week?
14. What content did my audience save—and why?
15. How will I recover from a wobble quickly?
16. What do I want to be known for in six months?
17. What will future-me thank me for doing today?
18. Where can I serve without expectation?
19. What evidence shows I'm already helping?
20. What will I stop, start, and continue this month?

Glossary

Visibility:

The practice of showing up where your ideal clients can see, know, and trust you.

Pillar Content:

Your top 2–4 core topics that anchor your message.

Signature Story:

A concise narrative demonstrating your values, transformation, and results.

Free Media:

Unpaid opportunities like podcasts, blogs, collaborations, and livestreams.

Organic Reach:

Visibility gained without paid advertising.

CTA (Call to Action):

A clear next step you invite your audience to take.

One-Liner:

A simple clarity statement: *I help [WHO] achieve [RESULT] without [PAIN], using [METHOD].*

MVV (Minimum Viable Visibility):

The simplest sustainable rhythm of showing up.

Closing Message

You don't need a team.
You don't need a following.
You don't need a budget.
You need your **voice**, your **story**,
and your **willingness to show up.**

Visibility is not loudness.
Visibility is ownership.
You were never meant to be hidden.
You were built to shine.
Your visibility starts now.

Want to keep the momentum going?

I invite you to join the **Show Up & Shine: Organic Visibility for Women Entrepreneurs** Facebook Group. A safe-and-supportive space created for women just like you who are ready to show up, share their journey, and build real visibility (without spending a dime). Inside you'll find encouragement, community, and simple organic strategies to help your voice be heard.

See you there — I believe in you. ♥

Author's Note

If this book supported you in any way, I'd love to hear from you. Share one line that resonated, one story you're ready to tell, or one visibility win—no matter how small—in the *Show Up and Shine* community.

Your voice might be the spark another woman needs today.

—Dr. Marcea B. Whitaker

Stay connected at www.drmarcea.com.

Made in the USA
Coppell, TX
30 January 2026